MW01173662

PIMP

Purpose In My Pain

COMPANION JOURNAL

DR. GWENDOLYN D. GIBBS

IBG Publications, LLC

PUBLICATIONS
Putting the POWER in your pen!

Published by I.B.G. Publications, LLC, a Power to Wealth Company

Web Address: WWW.IBGPublications.Com

admin@IBGPublications.Com / 904-419-9810

IBG Publications, LLC, Jacksonville, FL

Gibbs, Dr. Gwendolyn D.
PIMP: Purpose In My Pain, COMPANION JOURNAL

Printed in the United States of America.

P.I.M.P PURPOSE IN MY PAIN COMPANION JOURNAL

"Oh that my words were written!

Oh that they were inscribed in a book!"

– Job 19: 23

Made in the USA
Columbia, SC
18 June 2023

17907680R00057